THE
Archive Photographs
SERIES

IVYBRIDGE

The River Erme in winter showing Erme Road and mill chimney in the distance. London Hotel is on the right of the picture.

THE Archive Photographs SERIES

IVYBRIDGE

Compiled by
Ivor Martin
and members of the
Ivybridge and District Civic Society

CHALFORD

First published 1997
Copyright © Ivor Martin and members of the
Ivybridge and District Civic Society, 1997

The Chalford Publishing Company
St Mary's Mill, Chalford,
Stroud, Gloucestershire, GL6 8NX

ISBN 0 7524 0759 7

Typesetting and origination by
The Chalford Publishing Company
Printed in Great Britain by
Redwood Books, Trowbridge

Contents

PC (Slim) Richardson, showing Miss Emma Ann Wyatt across Fore Street on her 100th birthday.

Judges and committee members, Ivybridge Show, 1913.

Introduction

The town of Ivybridge lies on the edge of Dartmoor, at the start of the Two Moors Way. The remains of hut circles at Harford Moor tell us the area was inhabited by Stone Age people. Ivybridge is eleven miles from Plymouth and only seven miles from the nearest coastal seaside.

The River Erme runs through the town and is believed to be one of the fastest running rivers in the country, which is evident when the river floods. It is a natural habitat for brown and rainbow trout and salmon. Dippers make it their home as do kingfishers and is said that otters are making a come-back. The last one was killed in Erme Road by a local butcher but now within recent years there have been reports of them again.

It was due to the pure water of the river that the paper mill was established here which was really the start of the growth of the village. Before this the earliest mention of Ivybridge was of the actual bridge. Before the bridge was built it was the crossing for monks on their way between the abbey and monasteries at Tavistock, Plympton, Ashburton and was probably consisted of stepping stones or a small clapper bridge. The Duke of Wellington used the bridge on his way to Plymouth, when his horses were not ready he continued his journey on foot, walking and talking with the locals. When the coach caught up with him he declined the ride and the coach carried on without him. Then he arrived in Plymouth there was a reception committee waiting to welcome him.

Ivybridge became a town in 1977 with Jack Congdon being the first mayor. Ivybridge has certainly grown in recent years. From about 1850 to 1950 there were about 2,000 residents, but the late 1960s saw an increase to over 3,000 and now has over 16,000 residents. Ivybridge cannot grow any more without encroaching on its neighbours.

I hope you enjoy reading this publication as much as I enjoyed compiling it. When I first started, it was said that I would have a job finding 250 photographs, I have, but it was choosing the photographs from the many we already had plus others that have been given, with many new facts, whilst I was researching that was the most difficult. Perhaps I will be asked to compile a second selection, if there is a demand for it.

I would like to thank all those who have helped, the facts in this publication are believed to be true.

Ivor Martin
Ivybridge and District Civic Society
1997

One

The Bridge, River
and Woods

One of the earliest postcards of the bridge and certainly one of the most common examples.

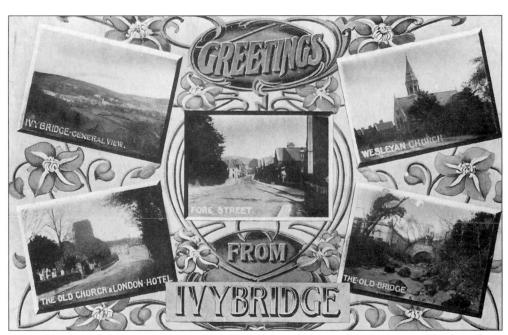

An early postcard showing five general views of the town, more of which you will see in later chapters.

Factory Bridge now under the flyover for the A38 Ivybridge by-pass. This bridge was blown-up in 1973. It used to carry the Ermington to Ivybridge Road. When it was blown-up the dust cleared and the bridge was still intact, so the whole process had to take place all over again. The by-pass was finally built nearly twenty years after the plans were passed.

The new bridge was built about 1826 to take the traffic over the River Erme, avoiding the old, narrow bridge. The tree in the right hand corner has since been removed after becoming infected with Dutch elm disease. A new disease-resistant elm was planted by the author, Barry Thorn and Jim Kelly as a replacement. Over 200 new trees have been planted in the town.

A recent photograph of the bridge which has been widened to convert it from a packhorse bridge to one able to carry stage coaches and other such vehicles. It is unclear when the alterations were made, but on careful study it would appear that this face of the view is a new one. The other side has still got a flame-holder attached to it.

One of the boundary stones on the bridge. These also acted as 'kicking stones' to stop stage coaches from hitting the original bridge.

The foot bridge that used to cross the Erme opposite the mill and a popular short cut from Harford. The remains can still be seen lying on the river bed. It would prove useful now for children from the community college and the Erme school to cross, saving traffic problems on the old bridge.

A leat gate to regulate water for Lees Mill water turbine, built by Mr Reg Vincent's grandfather. It can still be raised with the aid of a hand-forged spanner which was found in the River Erme by Lesley Martin.

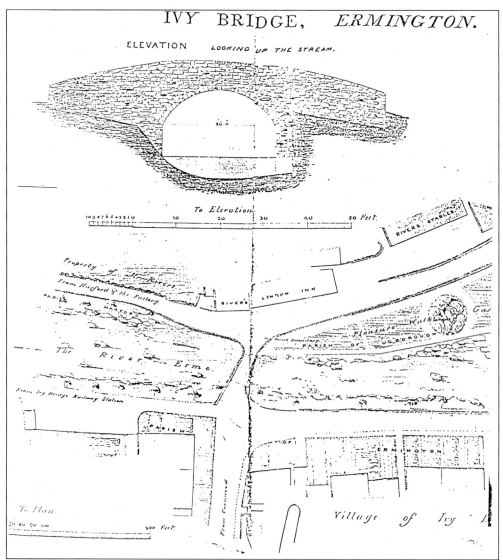

Plans of the bridge.

The gasworks on Keaton Road are visible at the bottom of the picture.

The A38 went straight through the town. The open space at the left is now Manor Way school and housing estate.

The town centre when the population was less than 3,000.

Ivybridge before the library and leisure centre were built.

16

Ivybridge during the 1950s. The building site on the far right of the picture later became the comprehensive school.

Ivybridge, before the health centre on Station Road and the temporary classrooms at the Erme primary were built.

LOVERS WALK, THE WOODS IVYBRIDGE. H.8

Longtimber and Pithill Woods. The woods cover about 53 acres and were acquired by the Town
Council in 1985 for the use of the townspeople and to save it from becoming a softwood
plantation. Now the wood is being planted with native hardwood and contains a very large
variety of fauna and flora.

On the E[r]me Ivybridge

Two views of the pleasant woods around Ivybridge, showing the River Erme and some local lads from about 1910.

A gentleman watches the river, 1906.

A walk in the woods, with the river on the right hand side, not far from the headweir.

Boys in the swimming pool (formally the village's resevoir), 1953. One of the boys, Len Beer, later became a botanist and travelled in the Himalayas.

A lady using the footbridge, 1907.

The woods in winter, photographed in the late 1800s.

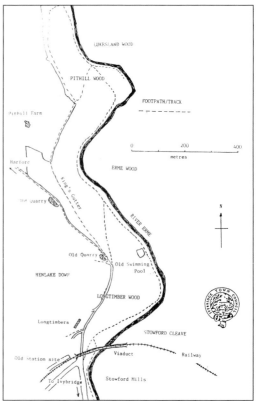

Map of Longtimber and Pithill Woods.

Two

Employment

Filham Silver-Lead Mine. The mine was situated in the fields south-west of Filham House, on the Ermington Parish boundary. Silver-lead was extracted before 1838, when the land belonged to Eton College. Mining continued with mixed success for 20 years, during which time the underground workings were extended and bigger and stronger machinery brought in. In 1856 the mine ceased to be viable, partly because of land ownership problems and work finally stopped. The machinery and other effects were auctioned off in July 1857. The photograph shows the massive engine house, already a ruin when the picture was taken. Steam power had been introduced in 1854 and when the mine closed, it had 2 engines, one a 24 inch horizontal 9 foot stroke, the other a 50 inch pumping engine with a 10 foot stroke, served by two 10 ton boilers.

A typical threshing scene showing the wheat being bundled into stacks in the 1930s.

A farm sale of cattle for John Stooke during the 1920s.

Farm sale at Sherford Farm for farmer John Stooke during the 1920s . The sheep are a Devon breed, the South Devon.

Devon School of Gardening, 1900. The school taught gentlewomen the art of horticulture and the gardens were where Stowford Mill garden is now.

The Devon longhouse in the 1880s. Note the horned-cows being milked by ladies in the yard.

Hay making time in the early part of the century. Note the pole lift and the firkin of cider in the foreground.

A local thatcher from the 1880s.

A lady carrying branches cut for hedging from Piles Copse.

A local farmers group outing to the BOCM depot in Bristol from Lee's Mill, 1949. The trip was made on an Ivybridge coach.

A trip to Weston-Super-Mare from Ivybridge, 1953. The name of the coach company is Hoare and Son (now Tally-Ho) and the driver is Sid Burring, pictured here with Alan Eastman.

A family cutting peat along the River Erme.

Stacking peat near Piles Hill, 1930s. Peat was used as a fuel in many farms on Dartmoor. The peat was dried before being transported off the moor.

Collecting bracken to be used as bedding for cattle, 1914.

A Dartmoor cottage, c. 1820.

Cutting granite for building, probably in the 1860s.

Dick Stephens from Park Street smithy with a thoroughbred horse. Note the docked tail which would not be allowed today.

Dick Stephens outside his smithy with Freddy Neave (right) and Mr W. Fry (centre), 1930s.

Dick Stephens (right) and Freddy Neave with their float for the silver jubilee of King George V, 1935.

Dick Stephens on his silver jubilee float, 1935.

Ivybridge viaduct was built to Brunel's design, between 1845-48. The line was converted to double track, standard gauge in May 1893 and the viaduct was replaced by the present stone and brick one on the south (downstream) side of the earlier one. Most of the stone pillars of the old viaduct remain.

Steam train passing through the new station, 1992. This was built with the aid of money from the EEC.

The brick and stone built viaduct is still in use today, but not this station.

Mr Winston, the earliest recorded postman in Ivybridge, photographed in the 1880s.

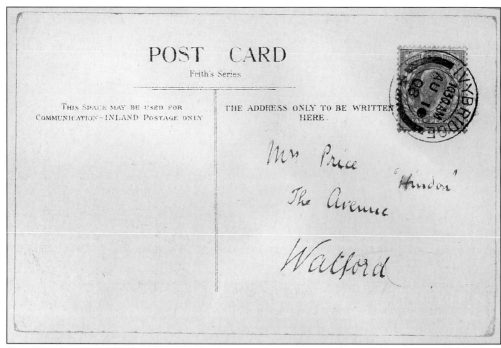

A postcard sent to Watford from Ivybridge, 10 August 1908. The first known use of the town handstamp in Ivybridge was in 1751. There are postal records for 1794, although there is no mention of a post office or postmaster.

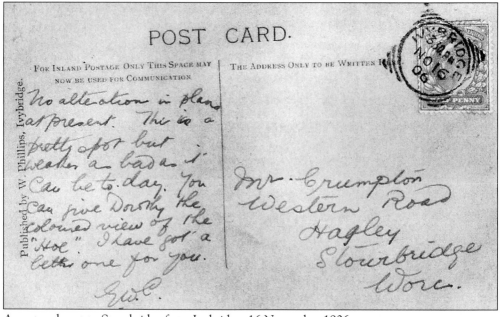

A postcard sent to Stourbridge from Ivybridge, 16 November 1906.

An example of a letter from Cornwood to Plymouth dated 28 December 1837. The boxed No. 1 was the Receiving House mark of Cornwood. The rate of 5*d* was charged to send such a letter and was made up of 4*d* for the journey from Ivybridge to Plymouth (a single sheet letter up to 15 miles) plus 1*d* for the Penny Post.

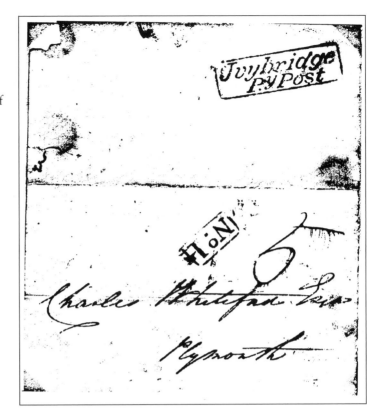

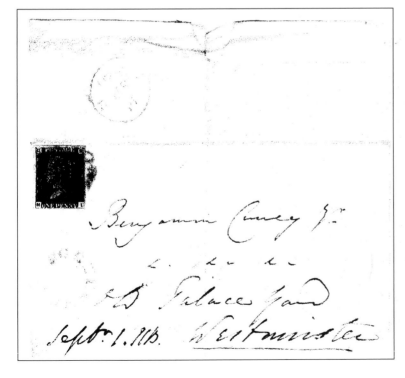

Letter from Fleet, Ermebridge dated 1 September 1840. The first known use of the office handstamp in Ermebridge was in 1829. This particular letter has a Penny Black and a red Maltese Cross. When the first 'adhesive labels' (the Penny Black) were issued on 6 May 1840, they were 'obliterated' by Maltese Cross handstamps using red ink.

MEMORANDUM.

FROM
W. Vincent,
Carpenter, Builder, Cabinet Maker,
and Undertaker,
WESTERN ROAD, IVYBRIDGE.
—o— ALL ORDERS PROMPTLY ATTENDED To. —o—

July 25 189 8

To *Mr G Smallridge*
Ironmonger &c
Ivybridge

Price for the erection of New Post Offices
at Nos 49 x 50 Fore street Ivybridge will be
the Sum of Seven hundred and thirty three
pounds Ten shillings
£ 733 „ 10. 0

Carpentering &c £ 274. 0. 0

W. Vincent & Rowse

A bill sent by W. Vincent, a builder from Western Road, Ivybridge, 25 July 1898. This is for the erection of the new post offices at numbers 49 and 50 in Fore Street, Ivybridge. The sum of which amounted to seven hundred and thirty-three pounds and ten shillings.

The post office at 50, Fore Street. The building was formerly a telephone exchange and also a dole office. It is now an estate agent's office.

The fire at the mill viewed from Mill Meadow, nowadays covered in houses.

The paper mill was first built here in the late 1700s, utilising the pure water from the River Erme. The water was also used to power the mill but this method is sadly no longer used. At one time all the paper for postage stamps was produced here as was the paper for the old white £5 notes. The mill caught fire on 5 May 1914 and was almost completely ruined but it was very soon back in production to the pleasure of many Ivybridge people. The mill was sold and taken over many times and is at present owned by Arjo Wiggins, a French company. It now specialises in fine quality and security paper.

The old and lower mill that produced 'half stuff' (part-finished paper) which was then transported to the top mill to be made into paper.

The horse and cart that was used to transport the 'half stuff' between mills.

Three
Winter Scenes

Lower Mill Leat, probably taken at the time of the great blizzard in 1891. This stone and brick-built leat carried water from the Erme to an overshot waterwheel which powered the paper mill in Keaton Road. In the left background there is the filter which cleansed the water used in the pulping process, from which part-finished paper was made ready for carting to Stowford Mill. In 1896 the waterwheel was replaced by a larger wheel, which was 18 ft in diameter with an 8 ft breast. Although somewhat rotted away, the waterwheel did survive until 1976 when it was removed to make way for Waterside House. The leat, however, still exists. In 1926/27, the old paper mill was sold to Ivybridge Electric Supply Co. who continued to use the water power for the supply of electricity to Ivybridge until the Second World War, when the old mill was burnt out, wrecking the generating plant. The photograph, one of Smallridges, was recognised by the late Mr Edwin W. Harvey in 1976, who provided the history.

The Bridge Inn following the blizzard of 1891. The walled garden belonged to the London Inn.

The Bridge Inn as it is today.

Stowford Lodge seen after the blizzard in 1891. The house was built by the Allen family who owned the Stowford Paper Mill.

The London mail train at Langham, March 1891. In 1891 the G.W.R. line to Plymouth was still Brunel's broad gauge and between Rattery and Hemerdon it was only single track, with passing places at Ivybridge and South Brent. On the 9 March 1891, the 6.50 am train from Plymouth, carrying over forty passengers, ran into problems due to the adverse weather conditions and passengers had to stay on board, overnight without food. The driver and one of the guards who went to raise the alarm reached Ivybridge in the late evening. On Tuesday morning a small party went to the rescue with a Mr Brown and Mr Greenhough in charge. They were working on the railway, preparing it for the change from broad gauge to narrow. On 12 March the train carrying the breakdown gang ran into the back of the one that had been derailed, killing one person and injuring a further two. A Colonel Rich blamed the driver, Nicholas Way, for the collision, stating that he should have satisfied himself of the correct position of the 6.50 train.

Young boys outside the Bridge Inn, after the blizzard of 1891. Note they do not seem to be well-equipped for such cold conditions. What about the caps? No self-respecting young lad would wear them now!

Six
Education

THE COLLEGES. &c · UNDER PATRONAGE OF · THE SCHOOL BOARDS

THE ELEMENTARY SCHOOLS PHOTOGRAPHING Cº. *Geo W Holden* MANAGER LEEDS & HULL.

Mr Lake with pupils of the Ivybridge Board School. He was head from 1873 and served for 31 years. It is said that by the time he retired he had personally taught most of the people in the town. During his term of office the pupil number went up from 140 to 370, higher than it is today. On his retirement he was presented with a purse containing £31.10.0 and an illuminated testimonial.

The Station Road Council School, now the Erme Primary School.

Mr Lake, the headmaster from 1873 to Christmas 1904.

Three girls from Ivybridge Board School, wearing some very smart dresses.

Miss Olver and Mr Alcock with children in the middle years of Ivybridge Board School.

Mr Luxton, the
headmaster in
1927.

A class of 10 to 11 year old pupils including Jessie Phillips, in 1926.

Girls evacuated from London during the Second World War. Gwen Pretty, Betty Thorn, twins Muriel and Joan Buxton, Miss Herring, Doris Lane, Yvonne Grist, Irene Jacques, Jean Phoenix, Rose Sargent, Alice Durrent, June Crow, Geraldine Travers. The twins came privately to stay with an aunt and all girls attended the school.

A Lynx helicopter visited school children and landed in Victoria Park, 1989. This was at the childrens request to help them with their camouflage project.

The pupils pictured with a tent bought with funds raised in aid of the Kurds during the Gulf War.

Mr George Close with a 1920 school group. Back to front: George Bray, Percy Morris, Arthur Northmore, Cecil Drown, Bill Bradshaw, Frank Tremlett, Frank Davis, Susan Hucker, Ivy Blight, Kath Brailey, George Naltrick, Maud Maddock, Tom Davis, Ivy Quirke, Kathleen Baber, Bessie Freeman, Audrey Lethbridge, Kathleen Fredrick, Lilian Davy, Maud Priddle, Grace Lowry, Mary Bowden, Phyllis Scoble, Tom Williams.

Entrance passage to the school, 1927.

R. Browning with others from the Board School at their garden in Bridge Park, 1926.

Tom Maddock became mayor of Ivybridge and was a local author. He was also governor of the Board School for many years.

Kathleen May and Ethel Ridge in the school play at Pound Farm.

The Lady Rogers School, Ivybridge was built in 1887 for the princely sum of £3,700 and is now converted into flats. Lady Rogers, the wife of Sir John Rogers (the Member of Parliament for Plymouth), died in 1766. She left in her will the sum of £10,000 on trust to be used, after the death of her husband, to set up and maintain a school for the education of 'poor, unfortunate children' of Devon and Cornwall. Sir John Rogers died in 1773, but it appears that the trustees were not able to put Lady Rogers' wishes into effect until 1787, when they rented a house near Plymouth and appointed a master and mistress at a salary of £30 per annum. This was to house up to 45 children between the ages of 8 and 18 years. In 1887, Lady Blatchford, a descendant of Hannah Rogers, presented the site at Ivybridge on which the old school stands. From then on, until after the First World War, the school trust was used for training orphan girls for domestic service, but it was found to be financially impossible to continue on these lines. In any case, the majority of these girls did not go into domestic service! The school buildings were then modernised and equipped to operate as an Orthopaedic Hospital School, the first of its kind in the south west. It was opened in 1925 under the supervision of the Ministries of Health and Education. By 1947 other orthopaedic hospitals and schools had been opened in the two counties of Devon and Cornwall, and following the introduction of the National Health Service, the trustees decided to seek new uses for the Trust Fund.

Dame Hannah Rogers School just after building at a cost of £90,000, in 1959. After negotiations with the Ministry of Education, with the local authorities concerned and with four other trusts, namely the Devon and Cornwall Female Orphanage, the Elize Hele and John Lanyon Educational Foundations and the Orphans Aid Trust, the school buildings were altered and adapted without resorting to public funds. In October 1949, the school opened for the reception of 27 children suffering from Cerebral Palsy. This time the school was not only the pioneer in the south west, but also only the fourth school for this purpose to be opened in the British Isles. On 1 October 1953, the Round Table movement in Devon launched an appeal known as the Fifteen Thousand Fund, sponsored by the Round Tables of Area 19 (incorporating the tables in the whole of the county of Devon) in commemoration of the Coronation of Queen Elizabeth II. The object of this fund was to provide an extension for the school to accommodate more children. This appeal eventually reached the astonishing figure of over £26,000 following of further negotiations with the Ministry of Education, the present school was equipped with accommodation for 50 children, as the first of its kind in the whole country.

Five
Religion

The front of the old Wesleyan chapel in Chapel Place. The building has been used as a school, court house and, in later years, the town hall. It was overseen by Mr R. Vincent, former mayor and local undertaker. The houses in front have now been removed and a shop sits in front of where they were. The building on the right is now an off-licence but was formerly the Co-op. The chapel is now a community centre.

Colonel Campbell, vicar of Ivybridge, 1920s.

A church parade at the turn of the century. The old church was then still intact.

The Ivybridge new St John's church, built and consecrated in 1882. This photograph was taken in August 1906.

Old church from the top of Blachford Road. The church was demolished in 1925 by Mr H. Blight for the sum of £5. The rubble was used to build houses at Bridge Park and at Blachford Road, which was then called Church Street.

The old vicarage now a private home. Before this was built, the chantry was the vicar's residence.

Interior of St John's church before the screens were put in. The inscription has now gone.

The old church hall, now a private house.

Blachford Road showing the old church, the White House (left) and Berberis (right), next to the Constitutional Club. Note the old gate which is still there today.

The view of the Congregational church from Exeter Road.

Interior of the Congregational church.

Hon F.B. Mildmay, MP for the Totnes
Parliamentary Division from 1885 to
1922.

Revd James Craig, minister of Ivybridge Congregational chapel around 1900. He lived for a while at the 'Fawns' at Ermington, a coaching house at one time, which is thought to be the location of this photograph.

Foundation stone for the Congregational church, laid by Hon F.B. Mildmay MP.

"Cadleigh House," Ivybridge.

Front view of the Priory. Cadleigh House Roman Catholic church, a Roman Catholic convent and school, were established early in the twentieth century.

Molly and Bill were the first to get married at St Austin's Priory, April 1947.

Methodist church and Allens cottages, 1900. The church and tower (95 feet high), together with the land, were valued at £4,000 and were given by the Allen family.

Mr John Allen laying the foundation stone, 15 July 1874. He was then duly presented with a silver trowel by architects Messers Norman and Hine.

Six
Old Prints of Ivybridge

A print of a peaceful scene in Ivybridge from 1791. This little known print is in the authors' collection.

A Roy Cooney engraving of the Ivybridge logo.

An early print of Ivybridge.

An early artist's impression of the mill.

The Grosvenor House was a coaching inn and later a doctor's house and surgery. The building is now used as an old peoples' residential home.

The London Hotel. The construction of this photograph is puzzling. Although it derived from a full-plate size photographic glass negative it seems to be part photograph and part drawing or brush work. How accurately it depicts the London Hotel at about the turn of the century is not known. The windows agree with those of the present frontage, except for the round topped window directly above this on the second floor level, which is not there any more. The roof and chimney stack agree fairly well.

Seven

The Redlake Clayworks

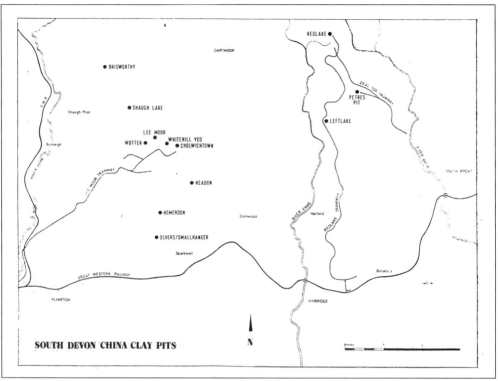

A map showing the South Devon China Clay Pits.

C.A. Hanson with manager Les Mutton in front. Behind them is the winding engine house. One truck is on the turntable at the top of the inclined plane.

The construction gang who laid the tramway, 1912-1914. The group includes Mr Matthews Senior, who was then living in Addicombe.

Redlake, 1920. In the centre is the engine house and to the right is the stores, carpenter's shop, blacksmith's shop, winch engine house and peat store.

Men loading sand from a sand-trap into a wagon. This is the only existing photograph of the bottom of the pit.

Jan Waye and Bill Warren Senior, shifting the overburden. Teams of three were employed and each team was paid by the fathom of peat shifted. Two men would cut and load the peat onto two wagons and a horse led by a boy would then take this to the tip.

Jan Waye, who ran Huntingdon Warren is shown here shifting the overburden with Violet the horse. Bill Warren Senior stands behind him.

The Sky Tip, 1926-30. A man at the top of the incline used a system of bells to signal to the man working the winching engine. From the bridge in the centre, sand could be tipped directly into wagons below on a branch line of the main tramway.

Construction of the stack of clay-dry or pan-kiln at Cantrell, 1910-1912. Granite from the redundant railway viaduct at Bittaford was used.

Settling tanks behind the kiln at Cantrell. The furnace is to the left, and beyond, is Cantrell signal-box which was removed in 1934.

Winding-engine house at the top of the inclined plane which faced closure in 1932. A make-shift boiler made from one of the scrapped engines is being used.

Linhay in which the dried clay is stored. This was shovelled through the loading bays into G.W.R. trucks in the siding below. In the centre is a weighing platform and on the right is the signal-box.

The pan-kiln with a travelling bridge. To the right, clay in settling tanks, was transported in wagons on temporary track onto the bridge to be distributed throughout the kiln. To the left, dried clay was shovelled into the linhay, a hot and steamy job!

Sinking of a shaft, 1912. On the left is a temporary engine shed and a Cornish beam engine was said to have been used.

The hostel which was run by Mrs Bray from North Filham, wife of George Bray, the Pit Captain. It housed about 40 men.

The remains of the hostel in 1981.

Harry Fox of Bittaford with *Dartmoor* at Redlake.

Dartmoor, a Ker-Stuart 0-4-2 Saddle Tank engine survived from 1911 to the works closure in 1932.

Carriages, one of three cut in half to make two short hen-coop-type cars.

Henry Fox with *Lady Mallaby Deeley* at Leftlake, taking on board snow for the boiler.

Redlake stationary engine house. Some peat, but mostly coal, was used as fuel to dry the peat.

Eight

Yanks in Ivybridge

The 11th Regiment of the Stonewall Brigade on parade, led by Captain 'Jack' Flora.

General Montgomery with Colonel Cannum of the 116th Regiment at Hanger Down, just before D-Day.

'The Pep Boys', Henry Housler, Moe (Bill) Caroniak and Mac (George) Gallagher at Harris Cottages.

October 1943. Left to right: Robert Blecker (killed in action), Milton Butt and Henry Housler.

Lt. Hannisfluck, known to his friends in Ivybridge as 'Baby Allan', wrote this poem about his memories of the war.

I want to go out to the moors again,
To retrace each painful stride,
To look again at the hills wherein,
The sheep and rabbits hide.
I want to go again to the moors,
To follow their winding trails,
To stand again on their lonely slopes,
In the cold and the rain and the gales.
Oh, I'll go out to the moors again,
But mind you and mark me well,
I'll carry enough explosives,
To blow the place to hell.

Captain 'Jack' Flora with Captain 'Zap' Zapacosta who was killed on D-Day.

Charles and Hester Lyttle. 'I was a member of Company A, 116th Infantry, 29th Blue and Gray Division that sailed from New York Harbour in September 1942, on the *Queen Mary*. This was the trip that the *Queen Mary*, when approaching England, destroyed a small destroyer ship that was criss-crossing in front of it. I was on the *Queen Mary* at that time. After arriving in England, we were sent to the Tidworth Barracks. After a period of time there, we were sent to Ivybridge for quite some time.

Before we left the States, I had been transferred from K Company to A Company as the Company Clerk. Then while at Ivybridge, I was transferred to the Regimental Headquarters as the Personnel Clerk of A Company. Bernard Harper who was the Personnel Clerk for B Company, became my best friend all through the war period. We visited a number of places and made a lot of friends, especially in Ivybridge. These included the Phoebe Phillips family, the Andrews family and the Betty Lang family, among others. A number of field trips were made out onto the 'Moors' as well as some hikes of twenty miles in one day. The time came for our move to Bournemouth in England and preparations were made for the 'D-Day' invasion. From that time on we were moving quite frequently until the end of the war in Germany.'

Charles Herbert Lyttle.

On the right is Captain Bedell in Germany, 1945.

The 116th Regiment on parade to receive their D-Day Presidential Citation.

Lt. Col. Tom Dallas.

Members of C Company, 116th Regiment, 29th Division.

Reunion of the C Company, 8 June 1992. Back row, left to right: Lawrence C. Lawson, Allen Z. Emswiler, Carlos J. Bennington, Benjamin F. Dean, Joseph F. Gambill, Norman Taylor, Carl H. Clutterbuck, Charles W. Ham. Middle row, left to right: Henry E. Miller, Raymond Scheurer, Robert J. Bedell, Edwin O. Hering, Weldon Huffer, Irvin F. Nash, Charles T. Hart, Joseph R. Bennington. Front row, left to right: George W. Homan, William E. Bryan, Leo A. Patterson, Claude Wine, Charles C. Baker.

OMAHA BEACH   116TH INFANTRY REGIMENT LANDING AREA   D-DAY 6 JUNE 1944

	CANNON CO.	MEDICAL DET. (WYTHEVILLE/ STAUNTON)	ANTI-TANK CO. (ROANOKE) 29TH SIG. CO. (NORFOLK)	ANTI-TANK CO. (ROANOKE) 111 FIELD ART. (RICHMOND, NORFOLK, PORTSMOUTH)	0820 5TH WAVE
		HQ 116TH (STAUNTON) HQ CO. 116TH (ROANOKE)	HQ CO. 3RD BATT. (WINCHESTER) M CO. (EMPORIA)		0730 4TH WAVE
	C CO. (HARRISONBURG) HQ 1ST BATT. (BEDFORD) D CO. (ROANOKE)	K CO. (CHARLOTTESVILLE)	I CO. (WINCHESTER)	L CO. (STAUNTON)	0720 3RD WAVE
2nd RANGERS	B CO. (LYNCHBURG)	H CO. (MARTINSVILLE)	H CO. (MARTINSVILLE) HQ CO. 2ND BATT. (ALTAVISTA) HQ 2ND BATT. (VICTORIA)	H CO. (MARTINSVILLE)	0700 2ND WAVE
	A CO. (BEDFORD)	C CO. (FARMVILLE)	F CO. (SOUTH BOSTON)	E CO. (CHASE CITY)	0630 1ST WAVE

CLIFFS

B E A C H

VIERVILLE DRAW   1ST PENETRATION   LES MOULINS

This map, drawn in 1984 by Robert Flory, shows the plan for the 116th Regiment Combat Team's assault on Omaha Beach, D-Day confusion actually scattered several of these companies away from their designated landing areas.

Landing Plan for the 116th Infantry Regiment on Omaha Beach, 6 June 1944.

Nine
Fore Street

Fore Street, 1990. This photograph was taken just before Glanvilles Mill was built, the area is now pedestrianised. Fore Street as we now know it, is a depleted shopping area compared to what it was in recent years. It used to support many more retail outlets and services, including three block units, garage, builders merchant, electricians, five butchers (all doing their own slaughtering behind their shops). The last butchers to do this was Pearses. Dewhursts has since closed and the premises is now a solicitors office. Mr Salters shop (now Whitfields) was a drapers where you could buy almost anything, up to the early 1970s. There was also a library within the premises but not the public one, this was housed in various locations including Station Road School, the Bridge Inn and Hawthorn House, where it occupied one small front room which operated well into the 70s.

At least three shops had bakeries. Bryants was one of these. They used to deliver by horse and trap and these had to go through the hallway to get behind to the stable. The trap was too wide so two chunks were cut out of the door to let the hubs of the wheels pass through. Town Dairy was a farm where the cattle were milked and the milk sold through the shop. Hawthorn House was also once a dairy. The Gallery and Shoe Repair Shop were once Luxtons Ironmonger and General Store. Mr Luxton would try and make it for you if he didn't have it in stock. Once again the business continued to run well into the 70s, up until Mr Luxton's retirement in fact. When the shop was converted, dynamite was discovered which was in a terrible condition and as a result the bomb squad were required to dispose of it. Mr Luxton used to deliver a cement mixer which he pulled behind his old Rolls-Royce car, which retired with him to Cornwall. There has been a lot of debate over which is the oldest business in Fore Street, but suggestions include D. Pearse or Friends, who have now moved. Dennis Pearse is himself the oldest trader, three generations of his family have now been trading in Ivybridge.

F. J. WHIDDON
(Late E. HENLEY),

41, Fore Street, Ivybridge

41 CENTRAL WHIDDON'S STORES. 41

FAMILY GROCER & PROVISION MERCHANT.

TEA & COFFEE SPECIALIST.

Tea Specially Blended to suit the Local Water.

An advertisement for F.J. Whiddon, one of the many grocers once in the village which have all now been replaced by just two supermarkets.

The Co-op General Store, which is now a wine merchants.

Babers the saddler, whose descendants are still living in the town. The shop stood where the rear entrance to Glanvilles Mill is now. Glanvilles Mill shopping centre was finally built in the late 1980s after many years as a corn mill. From about 1850 it was originally called Union Mill and was taken over by Henry Fice Lee in the early 1900s, who ran the premises as a corn-grist mill. He sold coal and coke and even generated electricity from here for the town. The large wooden bridge over the Erme bears a plaque dedicated to him. The mill was powered by water from the Erme. Water was diverted in Erme Road and under Fore Street into the mill by the entrance where lorries now enter. The turbine has been saved and is now in the car park on Harford Road (it looks like a giant snail). One elderly resident informs me that a pig once became trapped inside it! A lot of the older residents remember the mill with fondness. Twice weekly a travelling picture show came to the village and set up in the mill to show, in those days, silent movies, accompanied, of course, by a pianist, Miss Queenie Peline who was also a school mistress. Bill Bowden, for many years a mechanic and part-time fire chief for Ivybridge, tells how the local lads held an evening out for about 6d, going to the film, buying a stick of liquorice and taking a pea shooter with them. They used the loose grain and maize on the floor of the mill to shoot at people in the front rows! Eventually the manager would turn on the lights and proceed to throw them out. Other seats ranged from 6d to 1/3d. The mill was finally pulled down one Saturday morning in 1978 by the South Hams District Council. After many disappointments Ivybridge eventually gained a new shopping centre. At the other end, by Dennis Pearse the butchers, there used to be John Friends garage and before that his grandfather had a blacksmiths shop on this site. In the past this area was once a tannery and a brick-built pit has also been located on the site.

Allens Cottages built by Allens for workers in the paper mill. The road was then just earth and when a person in one of he cottages was very ill, the road was strewn with straw to stop the noise from cart wheels disturbing him. The council employed a Mr Williams to clean mud and horse muck from the road in inclement conditions. Marley the tailor's shop later became a bicycle shop, hardware shop and is now a Chinese takeaway.

Here we see the premises as a bicycle shop, on the right is the dairy. Cows were still being driven through the archway for milking within the last 50 years.

This photograph is looking in the opposite direction to the previous one, 1914. The mud road is still evident. The caravan is probably from the settlement at Westlake.

Looking up Fore Street from Glanvilles Mill entrance. On the right is the Kings Arms which later became the Fighting Cocks and is now the Exchange. Henry Fice Lee, Chair of Council, used to hold emergency meetings near this entrance under the oak tree (not visible in the photograph). Also, on the right was the home of William Crossing the Dartmoor writer.

Ten
People, Places and Events

Carnival Queen Amanda Kemsley with the Grumbleweeds at Dame Hannah Rogers School. Attendants were Rachael Foster and Joanne Rooney.

Carnival Queen Pamela House, at Lockyer Street Hospital meeting an injured soldier in 1943.

Carnival Queen Amanda Kemsley with Louise Churchill from Plymouth Sound Radio, 1985.

Carnival Queen Nicola Cockings, 1976.

Lee Mill Hospital's winning carnival float 'Lee Mill Rules', with Big Marge and company, 1985.

Rachael Blackett and Sharon Whitfield on the Carnival Queen's float, 1977.

First prize winners, Tina Bennet and Lesley Martin with HMS *Ivybridge* just after the Falklands War.

VE Day – fifty years on! Di and Ivor at the community college commemorative exhibition.

A carnival in the 1920s. A Lee and Sons lorry from Lees Mill, the local miller.

A windmill in a carnival in the 1930s. Once again it is a Lee's lorry.

Pam House, the Carnival Queen visiting the children's ward at the Green Bank Hospital, Plymouth, 1943.

Amanda Kemsley, Ivor Martin, Mike Rooney, Rachael Foster and Joanne Rooney outside the old town hall, 1985. The uniforms were loaned by Captain Farr MBE and were formerly used on a replica of the *Mayflower*.

The carnival Queen with Alf Broom as Carnival King. The young boy watching is Clive Meathral.

Tug of War team, Ernie Cox, Frank Davies, Maurice Coker (trainer), Charlie Hart, Len Skelly.

The Mayor of Ajax with Joan Skinnard, 1985. The mayor came over here from Ajax in Canada to collect a bell from a ship with the same name as his town. Usually a ship is named after a town, but this time the town of Ajax took its name from HMS *Ajax*. He was invited by the carnival committee to attend the concluding events and took part in judging and presenting prizes and awards to teenagers nominated for special efforts.

Ivor Martin, winner of the Edwardian evening in the Imperial Inn, pictured against the winning window display of Mike Lynn's hardware shop, now a shoe repairers and gallery.

An Edwardian evening at the Imperial Inn, Ivybridge, with Joe Lippett (landlord), Paula Wells (bar maid) and also Barry and Doreen Thorn. Ivybridge led Britain into Europe with a week long celebration including a visit from the twin town, St Pierre and a carnival. Ivybridge is the only town to request a donation of £400 from the government to help fund the events. A television programme was made for the occasion.

Charlie Tarr, an ex-policeman from Kingston sowing seed. He lived at North Filham and worked at farms in the neighbourhood of Filham and Ugborough.

John and Annie Pearse at the turn of
the century. They are at 'Tor Peek' in
Ugborough, where they lived until
1903, when they were succeeded by
their son Robert.

Mrs Lavers at home in Bittaford in the late 1800s.

Mrs Clarice Bowker showing the Maundy money she received from the Queen in Exeter cathedral for services to the church, 1983. She was a member of the Stone family of Erme Road.

James Murray Strickland who married Betty Harvey. He was a pilot in the Battle of Britain and killed in an accident at Portreath, Cornwall in 1941.

Reg Kingsland and his mother outside the
mill, 1943. Her first husband died after
contracting TB in the First World War.

Maxwell Hislop's wedding at Highlands
House, 1930s. Their son is Sir Robin Hislop MP.

Western Road showing the Imperial Inn, formerly the Prince Albert.

The Sportsmans Arms in Exeter Road. The G.W.R. bus with solid-tyres is on its way to Millbay station. Fields can be seen beyond the bus.

The White House on Erme Road when it was the Womens Institute and meeting house. It is now painted grey and has a gate at the side. George Wynne the artist lived here and some of his pictures are in Plymouth Museum.

The Plymouth to Ivybridge via Plympton, solid-tyre bus. A very shaky ride indeed! The shop behind was Lee's the tailors which is now a betting shop. The Constitutional Club is at the end of the road. The tree was blown down in a gale.

'Nirvana', built by a tea planter when he retired back to England.

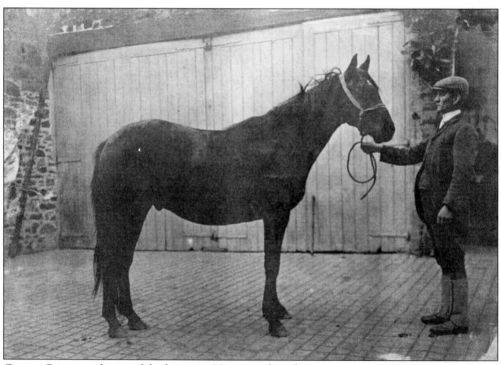

George Crimp, with one of the horses at Nirvana where he was groom, 1900. He eventually left here to work at Cornwood Blachford Estate for Miss Deare.

Longtimber Cottage, home of the late Freddy Hoare when he collected Smallridge plates. The house is a timber construction, once again built by a planter. The late Tom Maddock worked in the gardens as a young lad and saw them grow and mature. He then planted his own garden and was able to see that one develop too. Not many people can boast of such an achievement.

Mill Meadow soon after being built. The photo is taken from the rear, where bungalows for the elderly have now been built.

The naming of a road in Ivybridge called Rue St Pierre, after its twin town St Pierre Sur Dives in Normandy, 1972. Those present are, Reg Vincent (mayor), Digger Cooper, Chairman South Hams District Council, Joan Skinnard, John Eddy, Mike Jewers, Dave Lawrence. Cutting the tape is the mayor of St Pierre, Dr Paul Berl. The Rue St Pierre was officially opened in 1978. Ivybridge Parish Council decided to form a twinning link with St Pierre Sur Dives with the aim of promoting friendship across the channel. The council set up a committee consisting of interested bodies within the Ivybridge district, with a council representative to report back on the progress and activities of the newly formed Ivybridge and District Twinning Association. In 1974 Mr Colin Blackler, the chairman of the parish council, travelled to St Pierre to open a road called Rue de Ivybridge. Almost twenty-five years after its formation, the twinning association is still very strong and many long established friendships continue.

St Pierre Sur Dives the twin town for Ivybridge.

The River Erme, raging under the Ivy Bridge, the worst flood in living memory, 1992.

The river burst its banks at Erme playing fields, flooding the indoor tennis courts.

The London Hotel when it was known as Mallets Hotel, 1880.

A view of Ivybridge looking down river from Mallets Garden.

The entrance to the London Hotel in the 1930s. The building has since been converted into flats now known as London Court.

The front bar where many meetings took place and decisions were made.

Front view of the London Hotel just before its closure in 1991. The hotel dates from the late-eighteenth century and was always the social centre of Ivybridge. Many celebration in the town, such as laying foundation stones, seem to have been rounded off with lunch or tea at the hotel. When the hotel was sold in 1903 it was described as having 'coffee and commercial rooms, 5 sitting rooms, 15 bedrooms, spacious ball and assembly room and a well-accustomed public bar known as the London Tap'.

The Dartmoor Hunt leave via the Ivy Bridge in the 1920s.

The huntsmen enjoy a stirrup cup before setting off for the day, 1950s.

A meet at Stowford Mill with Edward Coryton, the master, 1910.

Huntsman sound the horn in honour at Susan Baker's wedding reception.

Dartmoor Hunt opening meet about 1900. Note the carriages in the background.

Meet at Highlands House. Ivybridge was the home of the Dartmoor Hunt for many years. People would come to stay here just for the hunting season but now the hounds are at Bittaford.

A hound show in kennels at Kennel Lane, a site which is now residential housing.

The Ivybridge song.

hours that are gone? O'er il - lusions by youth and by phanta-sy nurst? A - las! of the few that are

lingering, None wear the lights or the hues that en-circled the first. Oh, re-call not the past, though this valley be filled With

all we remember and all we regret, The flow'rs of its summer have long been distilled, The essence has perished : ah

let us forget!

Acknowledgements

This book has only been made possible with help from
Tony Barber, Charles Hankin and my family,
Lesley and Pauline, for putting up with me taking over the dining room.
Not forgetting Jackie, Terry, Di and all members of the Ivybridge and District Civic Society,
Mr Folley, Molly Bowden, Alec Rogers, Mike Lewis, Sheila Jewars, Roy Cooney,
Miss P. Phillips, Roger Morgan of Carne Frames and also,
Sue Bishop for her many hours of typing.